the Church of England and Christian–Jewish Relations

a contribution to a continuing debate

CHURCH HOUSE
PUBLISHING

Church House Publishing
Church House
Great Smith Street
London
SW1P 3NZ

ISBN 0 7151 5546 6

GS Misc 633

Designed by Visible Edge

Type size: 9.5/11

Printed by The Cromwell Press,
Trowbridge, Wiltshire

Published 2001 by Church House
Publishing on behalf of the Inter Faith
Consultative Group of the
Archbishops' Council.

contents

preface

Within the Church of England, there is a very wide range of passionately held, and in some cases irreconcilable, opinions about Christian–Jewish relations and connected issues. This document is offered to the Church as a resource to help identify what are the key questions involved, and to suggest ways forward for Anglicans in developing good relations with Jewish people. It does so by highlighting important areas of consensus within the Church of England, and suggesting positive ways forward on the basis of these. At the same time, the document also frankly describes areas of continuing disagreement among Christians. So this is both a hopeful and an honest piece of work, drawn together by a diverse group of Anglicans in consultation with individuals and organizations representing a still wider spectrum of positions.

It is important to be clear in three respects about the character of this document. Firstly, for reasons explained in Appendix 1, it presents specifically Church of England perspectives. It is not the result of a joint working group from the Jewish community and the Christian churches ecumenically, and in this it differs from the 1994 publication by the Churches' Commission for Inter Faith Relations, *Christians and Jews: A New Way of Thinking*.

Secondly, it is the Christian side of Christian–Jewish relationships which is the principal focus here. Given its necessarily limited scope, and its Christian authorship, the document does not presume to address the many key issues in contemporary Jewish life which are equally important in shaping the encounters of Christians and Jews.

Thirdly, as the title indicates, what is offered here is 'a contribution to a continuing debate'. This does not come as a definitive statement of Church of England attitudes.

Given the strength and diversity of feeling aroused by the issues with which it deals, this document has not been easy to write; its significance is all the greater for that. I commend it for discussion in the belief that it provides members of the Church of England with a good basis for advancing our thinking and practice in Christian–Jewish relations at the start of a new millennium.

✠ Thomas Southwark

acknowledgements

Several people have played a part in the writing of this document, as explained in Appendix 1. Particular acknowledgement needs to be made of the work of the members of the original working party of the Inter Faith Consultative Group:

The Revd Colin Chapman
The Revd Canon Dr Christopher Lamb
Dr Jenny Sankey
The Revd Dr David Rayner
The Revd Dr Walter Riggans

and of suggestions made during revision by:

Mrs Jane Clements
The Revd Dr Martin Forward
The Revd Jonathan Dean
Dr Anne Davison
The Right Revd Richard Harries, Bishop of Oxford.

I am also grateful for the many helpful comments offered by colleagues in the staff of the Board of Mission.

Permission to quote extensively from *Christians and Jews: A New Way of Thinking* (CCIFR, 1994) has been granted by the Secretary of the Churches' Commission for Inter Faith Relations.

Michael Ipgrave
Inter Faith Relations Adviser
The Archbishops' Council

introduction

Inter faith relations, and particularly relations between Jews and Christians, became the subject of sustained historical analysis and theological reflection during the latter part of the last century. All churches were greatly influenced by the Second Vatican Council's *Declaration on the Relation of the Church to Non-Christian Religions* (*Nostra Aetate*, 1965), which particularly urged dialogue and co-operation between Christians and Jews, and condemned all forms of antisemitism.[1] When at the 1988 Lambeth Conference the bishops of the Anglican Communion similarly endorsed the document *Jews, Christians and Muslims: The Way of Dialogue*, calling for 'understanding, affirmation and sharing', they were also building on the earlier work of pioneers such as the Anglican priest James Parkes. He had both developed a new Christian theological understanding of Judaism and confronted the difficult issue of antisemitism in relation to the New Testament.

Addressing the British and Irish situation, in 1994 the Churches' Commission for Inter Faith Relations published *Christians and Jews: A New Way of Thinking*, a document which was itself the product of a joint Jewish and Christian working group. The present paper draws extensively on that report. More recently, within the Church of England in particular attention has been drawn to the witness of Christians of Jewish origin. It is this latter development which provided the starting point for the present work; but it soon became clear that questions arising from the position of Jewish believers in Jesus can only be addressed within the broader context of Christian–Jewish relations. Moreover, while our focus is primarily on those relations within England, we are aware of the inadequacy of any treatment of the issues which restricts its scope to this country, or to western Europe.

This paper is therefore presented as a contribution for carrying forward a growing tradition of reflection and debate. A more detailed explanation of the background outlined above and of the document's nature is given in Appendix 1. It will be clear from the process there described that in some areas our task has been to present a continuing range of different attitudes and opinions to Christian–Jewish issues within the Church of England. Within the scope of this short paper, we have sought to clarify the fundamental issues at stake, not to resolve them. At the same time, we have also been able to identify important points where a consensus does exist. For continued growth in the Church of England's understanding of this complex and significant area, we believe that it is necessary both to recognize the divergences and to affirm the convergences.

chapter 1

the historical and theological context

In order to grasp the contemporary dynamic of Christian–Jewish relations, to find an adequate framework for interpreting New Testament attitudes to the Jewish people, or to approach from a Christian viewpoint key aspects of the modern Jewish experience (such as antisemitism, the Holocaust, or the State of Israel), it is necessary to have some historical and theological appreciation of the 'parting of the ways' between the two faiths.[1] This section is based on the chapter with that title in *Christians and Jews: A New Way of Thinking.*

the first century

By the end of the first century, profound changes had taken place in Jewish life with the emergence of a variety of religious groups, among which the Christians formed one. The loss of the Jerusalem Temple in the year 70 marked the end of the influence of the Sadducees with their Temple-orientated theology. The failure of the revolt of Simeon bar Kokhba (132–135) effectively finished the militant nationalist (anti-Roman) tradition represented by groups such as the Zealots.

Rabbinic Judaism was systematized during this time on the basis of ancient traditions and methods of biblical exegesis nurtured by the Pharisees. At the heart of the Rabbis' teaching was belief in the unity of God who, in covenant with the people of Israel, had chosen to give them his *Torah*, the divinely inspired teaching which forms the guide to every aspect of life: belief, ritual, ethics and social conduct. This faith included belief in the coming of Messiah, in the resurrection of the dead, and in the calling of the Jewish people to be a light for the Gentiles.

diverging theologies

Neither Jesus himself nor his first followers saw themselves as breaking with Judaism. Clearly, in the period leading up to his crucifixion Jesus was in severe conflict with the Jerusalem authorities, yet this struggle remained internal to Judaism. However, conflict soon arose between the Jewish and Gentile 'branches' of the nascent Church (Acts 15), and by not later than the second century Judaism and Christianity had separated into two distinct faiths. Why did this happen?

Many issues were involved in the rupture. Some were social, such as the division between Jews and Gentiles, the relationship with Rome, and the use of different stories and symbols in their respective communities. Social 'distance' increased after the destruction of the Temple by Roman soldiers in 70. Christians came to interpret this as God's rejection of Israel, and began to think of themselves as the 'new Israel' which replaced the old.

Then there were theological factors – for example, questions concerning the centrality of Jesus Christ, the interpretation of scripture, the abrogation or continuing validity of laws relating to the Sabbath, to circumcision, to food and drink. Jews and Christians began using biblical concepts like 'Messiah' and 'salvation' in different ways from each other. The Christian community developed Incarnational and Trinitarian theologies, which seemed to them inescapable implications of the faith of the Scriptures, highlighting and focusing the lengths to which God goes in his love of humanity. To Jews, on the other hand, such beliefs seemed to confuse the purity of belief in the unity and sovereignty of God. The attitudes of mutual hostility – not only theological, but also cultural, social and political – with which the two faiths finally diverged onto separate paths left their mark on both communities. Alongside the violence of much early Christian polemic against Judaism, for example, can be set the introduction into synagogal liturgy of formulae designed to exclude Christians.

While we cannot deny the significance of these questions which divided and still divide Jews and Christians, we must also be aware of the scriptural, theological and historical factors which they have in common.

the Torah

The Rabbis distinguished between the 'written' Torah (the Hebrew scriptures, including the prophets) and the 'oral' Torah, the latter being the interpretations and traditions believed to have been passed down by word of mouth from teacher to pupil since the days of Moses. A collection of these, compiled in Hebrew in Galilee around 200, came to be known as the *Mishnah* ('repetition'). Further reflection over the next three centuries resulted in the *Talmud*, the main text of Rabbinic Judaism (recorded in Aramaic). Two Talmuds exist, the Babylonian, considered to be the more authoritative, and the Palestinian (or Jerusalem) Talmud, compiled mainly in Galilee. The material of the Talmud takes the form of both *Halacha* and *Haggadah*. Halacha treats topics from a prescriptive, legal standpoint, whereas Haggadah is more discursive, often focusing on theological and ethical issues. The Babylonian Talmud, a vast work of some six thousand folio pages, has provided the foundation for spiritual reflection and deepening faith over the centuries for Jews throughout the Diaspora. Through such reflection Judaism has remained a living and evolving faith, even through the periods of great persecution.

It is important to recognize that these significant developments in Judaism took place after the time of Jesus, in the same centuries that Christianity itself was being formed. From this perspective, both Christianity and Judaism appear as contemporaneous religions, rooted in the Hebrew Scriptures.

Jewish contributions

Despite exclusion and persecution, Jews contributed actively to European culture throughout the Middle Ages. They also played a significant part in the Islamically ordered societies of Spain and the Middle East, where with Christians they were recognised as *dhimmi* ('protected people'). Indeed, in the course of history, the Jewish Diaspora has reached virtually every country of the world, with significant Jewish communities in places as diverse as China, Argentina, Australia, India, and South Africa.

As scholars and translators, Jews helped to mediate the learning of the ancient world, eventually, in Europe, helping to make possible the Renaissance and the birth of modern times. They were responsible for scientific and technological advances, such as astronomical tables, and were highly valued for their medical skills. The Jewish mystical spirituality of the *cabbala* fascinated Christian humanists such as Johann Reuchlin, who explored the interpretation of texts at multiple levels of meaning. Equally, Rashi (1040–1105) and other Jewish Bible commentators greatly influenced the Reformation 'rediscovery' of the Hebrew scriptures, with its emphasis on literal exegesis.[2] The greatest Jewish thinker of the medieval period, Moses Maimonides (1135–1204), practised and wrote medicine, but his most lasting achievement was in law and philosophy; his harmonization of Aristotle and the Bible influenced St Thomas Aquinas and other European philosophers and theologians.

persecution

Jews in Europe (and to some extent in North Africa and the Middle East) have never been far from persecution. At the end of the eleventh century the first Crusaders killed Jews as they made their way from Europe to the Holy Land. Later, Jews were blamed for the Black Death and consequently slaughtered. In Spain many were expelled or forcibly converted, and if they were suspected of retracting were burnt at the stake. Not only were they accused of being the 'killers of Christ', but malicious untruths were told about them, such as the 'blood-libel', according to which Jews would capture and murder a Christian child in order to use his blood in the baking of unleavened bread at Passover. This popular contribution to the myths fuelling antisemitism seems to have originated in England, but the libel soon spread through Europe.[3] The Jews were expelled from England by Edward I in 1290, only being allowed to return in 1656.

Jews were the target of Christian polemic in the writings of many church leaders and theologians both during the Middle Ages and in the Reformation era. From time to time they were forced to engage in public disputations with Christian theologians, with severe consequences even if they were successful in argument. The 'teaching of contempt'[4] led to discrimination and persecution, including exclusion from the ownership of land and from normal means of commerce, the enforced wearing of a distinctive badge, and separation into 'ghettos'. Misrepresentation and the caricaturing of Jews have been features of much Christian preaching in all churches, with the Gospels themselves being used to malign and denigrate the Jewish people.

continued reflection

Persecution has failed to rob religious Jews of deep joy in the service of God, or to divert them from constant reflection on the Torah. Like Christians, Jews have constantly striven to relate their faith to the evolving philosophies of the world, and to the present day continue with great vitality the exploration of their faith through the study of Bible, Talmud and later writings, affirming the relevance of tradition to the problems of the contemporary world.

chapter 2

the New Testament

the rediscovery of the Jewishness of Jesus

Christian and Jewish scholars like E. P. Sanders and Geza Vermes have done much in recent decades to place Jesus within the context of first-century Judaism. The work of CCJ (the Council of Christians and Jews, founded in Britain in 1942) and other educational organizations has enabled many Christians to appreciate the Jewish roots of the Christian faith.

anti-Judaism and antisemitism in the New Testament

Christian scholars have come to radically different conclusions on this issue. Gregory Baum, for example, in 1965 concluded that 'there is no foundation for the accusation that a seed of contempt and hatred for the Jews can be found in the New Testament' (Baum, 1965); yet by 1974 he had revised this opinion – in his introduction to Rosemary Radford Ruether's *Faith and Fratricide* (1974) Baum wrote that the earlier book 'no longer represents my opinion'. This brought him close to the position of James Parkes, who towards the end of his life had argued that: 'It is dishonest henceforth to refuse to face the fact that the basic root of modern antisemitism lies squarely in the Gospels and the rest of the New Testament' (quoted in Lloyd-Jones, 1993). Among the various scholarly approaches to this complex issue, we may distinguish three typical positions around which interpretations cluster. At the risk of introducing anachronistic categories of interpretation, it is important here to distinguish between, on one hand, hostility directed against Jews as a race and, on the other, attacks specifically focused on Jewish religious belief and practice. These two phenomena have come to be labelled as 'antisemitism' and 'anti-Judaism' respectively.

1 antisemitism rests on misinterpretation of the New Testament.

This was argued by Jules Isaac, a Jewish historian from France (Isaac, 1964; 1971). He coined the expression 'teaching of contempt (*l'enseignement du mépris*)' to denote those aspects of Church teaching which disparaged Jews and Judaism, for instance accusing Jews collectively of killing Christ, declaring them an accursed and rejected people, attributing exceptional vices to them collectively, and asserting that their religion had been displaced by Christianity.[1]

He saw such teaching, which was radically exploited by the Nazis, as primarily the responsibility of the later Church, arising from a failure to understand the true meaning of the New Testament. Similarly, Graham Keith, a Scottish Presbyterian from Ayr, suggests that Christians need to find ways of holding in balance both elements of Paul's teaching in Romans 11.28, namely the Jews' election, which is irrevocable, and their unbelief in the Messiah. The New Testament, properly understood, therefore contains an antidote both to anti-Judaism and to antisemitism (Keith, 1997).

2 antisemitism is inherent in the New Testament.

This is forcibly maintained, for example, by Rosemary Radford Ruether, an American Roman Catholic theologian (Ruether, 1974). She believes that the concept of 'sibling rivalry' can help to explain the violence of the attack on the Jews in the New Testament. Since anti-Judaism is so fundamental to the earliest Christian position, Ruether proposes that a radically new Christology is required in order to avoid it.

3 the New Testament's attack on certain expressions of Judaism can be paralleled in other Jewish writings of the time.

James Dunn, of the University of Durham, for example, challenged the belief that the New Testament is explicitly and deliberately anti-semitic by arguing that all forms of Judaism at the time of Jesus were vigorously and polemically pluralist (Dunn, 1988). Tom Wright, Canon of Westminster Abbey, takes a similar approach, speaking of 'the moment when some hitherto frightened and puzzled Jews came to the conclusion that Israel's hope, the resurrection from the dead, the return from exile, the forgiveness of sins, had all come true in a rush in Jesus, who had been crucified'. He goes on to say: 'This does not make Christianity anti-Jewish, any more than the Essenes, the Pharisees, or any other sect or group were anti-Jewish' (Wright, 1992; cf also Wright, 1993).

What is certainly clear is that scholarly interpretation of the New Testament must take seriously its Jewish context. Marcus Braybrooke, for example, an Anglican writer and thinker who has written extensively on Jewish–Christian relations, emphasizes that the titles used of Jesus arose first within the Jewish world and were used by Jews (Braybrooke, 1990). He furthermore points out that Jesus' message was centred not on himself but on the kingdom of God, and that Jesus leads us to the Father, the one God of all humankind. Gareth Lloyd-Jones, of the University of Wales, takes a similar view when he writes:

> Critical study of the Bible has emphasised the fact that the New Testament writings are historically conditioned and that the circumstances under which they were written impose limitations upon them . . . Consideration of the historical sayings not only helps to explain the hostility [to Jews found in the New Testament], it also helps us to recognise that the authors of the Gospels read back into the ministry of Jesus issues which applied to their own time, forty or fifty years later, when the Church and the Synagogue were rapidly parting company.[2]

chapter 3
antisemitism

The term 'antisemitism' was first used by the German journalist
Wilhelm Marr in 1879, deriving from terms coined by Ernest Renan
in a different context. It refers specifically to forms of prejudice
against Jews or Jewish beliefs, practices or customs. More properly
it usually relates to political and economic activity against Jews or
Judaism; other aspects are better referred to as 'anti-Judaism'.

It is however helpful to view the appearance of the phenomenon in
a nineteenth- and early twentieth-century European context. Jews
hoped for equality in the emerging democracies of modern Europe,
particularly in France and the German-speaking countries, after
centuries of discrimination and persecution. Two powerful myths
developed which undermined this ambition and are perhaps the key
constituents of modern antisemitism. The first was economic: it was
widely claimed that wealthy Jews formed a world-wide conspiracy
whose control of capital threatened all other economic activity.
Secondly, based ultimately on the racial theories of Gobineau, the
social and political ills of a particular state or country were attributed
to the corruption of its original Aryan purity by Jewish blood. While
this latter myth became most highly developed in Germany and
Austria, the events of history should not conceal the fact that for
Gobineau the ideal of Aryan purity was the French aristocracy.

While emancipation was granted to Jews in some countries, assimilation was generally regarded as the price Jews must pay for their
safety. However, events such as the Dreyfus case in 1894, when a
French army officer of Jewish origin was wrongly convicted of treason
in a blatant case of injustice, raised serious questions for many
European Jews about the validity of this approach. Later occurrences
in Russia and Germany proved that Jews, whether practising Judaism
or not, were always viewed as being in some way different, and generally that they suffered for it. It was in response to these feelings of
insecurity that the First Zionist Congress, convened by Theodor Herzl
in 1897, proposed the goal of a homeland in Palestine where the
Jewish people could be guaranteed a secure nationhood.

The 'Jewish question' (German *Judenfrage*) appeared as a concept
at least as early as the 1890s. Around it clustered a range of issues
which arose from the presence of Jewish communities of either

significant numbers or significant influence in the cultural, political and economic life of an overwhelmingly Christian Europe. It was a question explicitly discussed by Jews themselves, reflecting openly for example on the merits and demerits of assimilation. There was also a literature written by sophisticated, western-European Jews about the 'problems' caused by the large Jewish population of central and eastern Europe, many of whom were regarded as an ignorant and superstitious embarrassment for a community seeking acceptance and equality in society.

Somewhat anachronistically, the term 'antisemitism' is also sometimes applied to earlier anti-Jewish prejudice. Already in the classical world, Jewish refusal to assimilate aroused distrust, slander and occasional persecution – experiences which came to be shared by the early Church. In patristic Christianity, accusations of moral degeneracy and religious obduracy took precedence over such criticisms of anti-social behaviour. Christian hostility to Judaism was prominent in the monastic movement. It reached a frightening level of intensity in John Chrysostom's eight *Homilies against the Jews* (386–7). The specific context of his vituperation reflects anxieties over a resurgent Judaism which proved attractive to many in the Antioch of his time, yet its lasting legacy can be seen in the persistence of a current of antisemitism in some parts of Eastern Orthodoxy up to the present.[1]

For the significant communities of Jews living in Western Europe throughout the Middle Ages also, rights and privileges were generally restricted in law. Examples of outright persecution were frequent enough and the prejudice was almost universally of religious origin.[2] Relations between the authorities (whether civil or religious) of 'Christian' Europe and Jews, who were portrayed as having murdered Christ and rejected God, have continued to be precarious into the twentieth century. The taunt to Jewish children that they 'killed Jesus' may still be heard in British playgrounds today (for a survey of contemporary antisemitism in Britain, see the Runnymede Trust's *A Very Light Sleeper*, 1994).

This history of intolerance made the European churches profoundly vulnerable to the racial and social theories of modern antisemitism, which often blended subtly with the older prejudices in church teaching. As noted above, this can sometimes be observed in the liturgies for Holy Week, as well as in popular Passiontide devotion. The Roman Catholic Church in 1985 addressed these issues in the Vatican Commission's *Notes for Preaching and Catechesis*, and the 2000 Oberammergau Passion Play has been revised in a bid to overcome the antisemitic character of earlier versions.[3] Most significantly, at the outset of a new millennium, and immediately before his pilgrimage to Israel/Palestine, Pope John Paul II marked the First Sunday of Lent (12 March) 2000 as a 'Day of Pardon', in which – in the name of the Catholic Church – he asked forgiveness for the 'faults of the past'. The fourth of the seven sections of the Pope's 'Universal Prayer' was a 'confession of sins against the people of Israel'. John Paul II's words were as follows: 'We are deeply saddened by the behaviour of those who in the course of history have caused these children of yours to suffer, and asking your forgiveness we wish to commit ourselves to genuine brotherhood with the people of the covenant.'[4]

chapter 4
the Holocaust

In the 1930s in Germany the Nazi party led by Adolf Hitler came
to power. Hitler, a believer in the racial theories supporting 'Aryan
supremacy', was obsessed by the concept of the 'purity' of the
German people. Many groups suffered as a result; but the most
dramatic action was against German Jews, most of whom were
proud to be German and many of whom had fought for their country
in the First World War. A series of petty restrictions became full-scale
anti-Jewish laws, forbidding them from playing any role in society.
Finally, all those of Jewish descent or background who came under
Nazi control in Europe were sought out. At the Wannsee Conference
in 1942, the 'final solution' (*Endlösung*) to the Jewish question was
enacted: the ultimate destruction of all Jews. Special 'facilities' for
this mass murder were built and utilised by the Nazis. It is estimated
that around six million Jewish men, women and children perished.

Contemporary research into the Holocaust, and reflection on its
significance, continues vigorously. Many aspects of its history, its
current commemoration, and its philosophical or theological interpretation arouse great controversy. It may be seen as a particularly
pernicious racist episode or as an act of genocide on a grand scale.
This is to put it in a category to which other acts of organized terror
belong. In terms of sheer numbers the transatlantic slave trade and
the Stalinist purges far exceeded the Holocaust. What makes many
see the Holocaust as unique is the deep sense of rejection and
hatred shown towards Jewish people by the Nazi party and their
sympathizers, and the widespread compliance of the German nation.
For some this means that the Holocaust is not finally explicable in
the categories of racism or genocide. The claim of some scholars
should be noted, however, that Hitler was impressed by the Turkish
massacres and exiles of Armenians and Assyrians.

The variety of Jewish responses to the Nazis' genocidal project
can be seen from the Hebrew words used to describe it. *Shoah*
('calamity') emphasizes the uniqueness of the event, whereas
hurban ('destruction') helps to locate it within the continuum of
Jewish history: as the third hurban, the Holocaust follows in the
sequence of the destructions of the First and Second Temples.
Probably the most influential Jewish response to the Holocaust

has been Emil Fackenheim's insistence that to the traditional enumeration of 613 commandments in the Torah there should now be added one more – number 614 – which is in four parts: first, to survive as Jews; second, to remember the martyrs of the Holocaust; third, never to deny or despair of God; and fourth, never to despair of the world 'as the place which is to become the kingdom of God'. To abandon any of these imperatives, Fackenheim insists, would be to hand Hitler posthumous victories (Fackenheim, 1982).

The Nazis viewed Christianity and the churches with deep suspicion. Nevertheless, in spite of many individual acts of heroism and the principled resistance in some areas of the Confessing Church, the churches at the institutional level in general were compromised and appear at times to have colluded with the regime of the Third Reich. While the literature on the history of the Holocaust is immense, much more needs to be done by Christians on its theological implications. What has been done generally addresses the question of how the providential love of God can be reconciled with the Holocaust. The churches are beginning to examine their own role in relation to the Holocaust and the contribution to it of the theological legacy of Christian intolerance in the past.

One recent response from the Roman Catholic Church has been the document produced by the Vatican Commission for Religious Relations with the Jews, *We Remember: A Reflection on the Shoah* (March 1998). Described by Cardinal Cassidy, one of its authors, as 'an act of repentance ... more than an apology', this calls for a 'moral and religious memory' on the part of Christians and 'a very serious reflection on what gave rise to it (the Shoah)'. Out of a recognition that Christians 'were not strong enough to protest' at the disappearance of Jewish neighbours, there is a call for repentance: 'We deeply regret the errors and failures of the sons and daughters of the church.' It ends, however, on a more positive note:

> We pray that our sorrow for the tragedy which the Jewish people has suffered in our century will lead to a new relationship with the Jewish people. We wish to turn awareness of past sins into a firm resolve to build a new future in which there will be no more anti-Judaism among Christians or anti-Christian sentiment among Jews, but rather a shared mutual respect . . . To remember this terrible experience is to become fully conscious of the salutary warning it entails: the spoiled seeds of anti-Judaism and antisemitism must never again be allowed to take root in any human heart.

The document has had a mixed response, with some Jewish groups in particular expressing a measure of disappointment. Their main criticisms have been that it is much weaker than some statements already made by the Pope himself; that it fails to address issues arising out of the 'silence' of Pope Pius XII; that while noting senior authorities who resisted the Nazis, it does not mention those who collaborated; and that the distinction between anti-Judaism and antisemitism is questionable.[1] On the other hand, the document has also been recognized as a significant contribution to the churches' continuing reassessment of Christian contributions to, and complicity with, Nazism. It is extensively quoted in the theological paper *Memory and Reconciliation*, which provided the theoretical background to Pope John Paul II's 'Day of Pardon'.[2]

In October 1999, the Home Secretary published Government proposals for an annual national 'Holocaust Remembrance Day' on 27 January to serve as a commemoration of the communities who suffered as a result of the Holocaust, an educational opportunity for this and subsequent generations, and a sign of a 'continuing commitment to oppose racism, antisemitism, victimisation and genocide'. The importance of developing this proposal on an inclusive basis has been stressed: the national memory needs to honour, alongside six million Jews, victims of other genocidal atrocities, and also other groups victimized by the Nazis – for example, Roma people ('gypsies'), Jehovah's Witnesses, homosexuals, and people with disabilities.

Meanwhile, the need to be vigilant in remembering the attempted eradication of the Jewish people is underlined by the continuing activities of the self-styled 'revisionists' who deny or minimize the Jewish Holocaust. In April 2000, the right-wing historian David Irving lost a high-profile libel case which he had himself brought against Professor Deborah Lipstadt for her criticisms of his work (Lipstadt, 1994). The detailed judgement delivered by Mr Justice Gray in this case provides a comprehensive analysis and refutation of the so-called 'revisionist' (more accurately, 'Holocaust-denying') position.[3]

chapter 5
the State of Israel

The significance of Israel for Jews is summed up by *Christians and Jews: A New Way of Thinking* (1994) in these terms:

> Israel is important to nearly all Jews as a vital focus of Jewish faith, as a culmination of an age-old longing, and as a place of security after centuries of persecution. Since World War II many churches have issued statements in which they recognise this imperative reality of contemporary Jewish life. They suggest that disregard for Israel's safety and welfare is incompatible with the Church's necessary concern for the Jewish people. Christians are therefore called to enter sympathetically into Jewish fears and hopes for Israel.

In a new relationship between Judaism and Christianity, Christian attitudes must start from an understanding of Jews as a people, and not simply as a religion. For most Jews attachment to the land of Israel is an essential aspect of their personhood, although some may regard emphasis on the Israeli State as a diminution of the heart of Jewish faith. This raises for Christians questions about the continuing validity of the promise of the land, and the extent to which that promise can refer to the present State of Israel; on these issues, where theology and politics are inextricably mixed, Christians hold widely differing views.[1]

the Palestinian issue

Christians and Jews: A New Way of Thinking goes on to describe the tension in the minds of many Christians between sympathy for the State of Israel and solidarity with the Palestinians:

> But Christians also have to balance this with acute concern for justice for the Palestinian people, many of whom are Christian – Anglicans, for example, feel a particular bond with the predominantly Arab Episcopal Church of Jerusalem and the Middle East.

It is significant in this regard that both the Archbishop of Canterbury, with his fellow primates of the Anglican Communion, and the Roman Catholic Archbishop of Westminster appealed in the Millennium year for support for the churches of the Holy Land.

The 1994 report continued:

> As an occupying power (in the West Bank and Gaza) the policies of Israel should be judged according to the standards of international law. Christians who criticise or support particular policies will be sharing in a continuous debate in the Jewish community itself, especially in Israel. If they are critical, they should refrain from attacks on the integrity and legitimacy of the State of Israel as such.

Some Christians would want to question the concept of a state based on race or religion, while maintaining that this is different from attacking Israeli integrity or legitimacy as such. The future of the Palestinian people as a whole raises major questions about structural justice, while the particular situation of Palestinian Christians (large numbers of whom have emigrated in recent years) is a story of pain and courage which churches in solidarity have to hear attentively. These are issues which have engaged many in the British churches with a particular urgency, as the recognition has grown that Christian presence within Arab societies has been disastrously weakened.

In their discussions with each other in Britain, Jews and Christians have to reckon with a situation in Israel and the Middle East that is constantly changing. Major factors which affect relationships at the time of writing include: the fragility of the peace process owing to the fierce debate within Israel and among the Palestinians concerning the handing over of land to the Palestinian Authority; wider tensions in the region, particularly those involving Iraq and its neighbours; and, perhaps most problematically of all, the difficult questions of the status of Jerusalem, of justice for all the city's inhabitants, and of free access to it for all people.

a complex question

Discussion of these issues arouses a great deal of passion among both Christians and Jews, and suggests that there are two opposite dangers that need to be avoided. Some, on the one hand, seem to downplay the importance of the conflict between Israel and the Palestinians, failing to recognize the seriousness of the issue in the minds of many on all sides of the conflict. Others, however, are in danger of attaching to this conflict too much significance for Jewish-Christian relations in this country.

It is important to recognize that Jews and Christians are frequently divided among themselves, both in the Middle East and here. Finding ways to contribute constructively to the search for justice and peace in Israel/Palestine is a major challenge in inter faith relations for all three Abrahamic religions; it is difficult to see how any dialogue on these questions could meaningfully proceed between Christians and Jews without the engagement of Muslims also. Furthermore, while members of the Church of England can and do hold strong opinions on these issues, their readiness to express their views should be tempered by the recognition that they do not have to live directly with the consequences, as do Arabs and Jews in the Middle East.

chapter 6
Jewish people who believe in Jesus

In an increasing number of inter faith situations, people find themselves participating at a deep level in different religious traditions while seeking to be followers of Jesus. Two examples from very different contexts would be Christian partners in inter faith marriages, and people from Hindu, Muslim, or Sikh communities who feel called to be disciples of Jesus while remaining somehow within their original religious context. These examples in different ways raise questions of whether, and to what extent, it might even be possible to 'belong' to another faith community as a Christian. Of course, this pattern, which has been called 'dual faith' membership, poses problems of defining identity not only for Christianity but also for the other faith involved; and nowhere are these issues more vigorously contested than in the case of the Jewish community.

In part, this is because, from a Christian point of view, Judaism stands in a unique relationship to the Church. The Christian faith is indisputably related to the Jewish people through our common roots: God, Scripture, the Messianic hope. The earliest Christian community of all was Jewish, and Jewish people who come to faith in Jesus as Messiah naturally wish to assert their continuing Jewish identity. On the other hand, Christian beliefs are radically different from those of Rabbinic Judaism, and the history of antagonism between the two faiths, the Jewish experience of Christian-inspired discrimination and persecution, and particularly the memory of forced conversions of Jews to Christianity all strengthen the insistence of the overwhelming majority in the Jewish community that clear distinctions must be maintained between Christian and Jewish identities.

The issues are complicated by differences over terminology. Over the generations, and in different cultural contexts, various self-definitions have been used by Jewish people who believe that Jesus is the Messiah. This is, of course, quite apart from terminology assigned to them by Jewish and Christian communities in accordance with their respective understandings. Before the Holocaust, the most common expressions were either 'Jewish Christian' or 'Hebrew Christian', and these terms are still to be found among many who wish to assert that they are at the same time both Jewish and Christian (e.g. Montefiore, 1998). Recently, however, a growing number of Jewish believers in Jesus have come to feel that such self-designations reflect a social context where believers had to change their lifestyles completely to be accepted by Christians. Those who feel in this way prefer to describe themselves as 'Messianic Jews', drawing attention to the fact, as they see it, that they are still definitely Jewish people, but Jewish people who believe that Jesus is the Messiah of Israel. For them, this is a term which speaks of identification with Jesus without suggesting any compromise of their Jewish identity. They believe that the inner religious significance of what it means to be Jewish is fulfilled through their relationship with Jesus as Messiah.

It does not seem appropriate for Gentile Christians to become involved in debates about which people are or are not qualified to describe themselves as Jewish, but it is important to be aware of the complexity of the issues involved, of the plurality of definitions of Jewishness within the Jewish community, and yet also of the massive rejection by nearly all (non-Messianic) Jews of the claims to authentic Jewish identity of Jews who have accepted Jesus as Messiah.[1] Ethnic, cultural, and religious factors all play a part in the overall construction of Jewish identity. Distinctions can also be drawn between denying that a person is a Jew in terms of fundamental identity, on the one hand, and denying that person the privileges of Jewish community membership, on the other; or, relatedly, between a theological and a communal sense of what it means to be Jewish. These apparently subtle points are significant, for example, in the administration of the Israeli 'Law of Return', which does not grant to professing Christians the access to citizenship which is available not only to other born Jews but also to former Gentiles converted to Judaism in accordance with Halacha.[2]

For the churches too, Jewish believers in Jesus pose a number of challenges. Many of them have understandably been enthusiastic in sharing their faith with other Jews, and this raises the question of mission, a variety of Christian views on which are outlined below.[3] A rather different set of issues is highlighted by the negative experiences of Gentile Christianity which many Messianic believers have had: antisemitism (it should be remembered that Jewish Christians were among those who suffered in the Holocaust), lack of appreciation of their Jewish culture, forced conversions. Conversely, Messianic congregations – some of which include significant numbers of Gentiles as well as Jewish believers – can be challenged about some of their positions also. There would be great value in furthering a dialogue between Messianic Jews and 'traditional' churches; Appendix 2 suggests some detailed questions which could be asked in either direction.

chapter 7

seven areas of agreement among Christians

It is possible to identify a number of important points in Christian–Jewish relations on which there is a developing consensus among Christians – and, in many cases, also between Christians and Jews. All of these, to varying degrees, require attitudes significantly different from those which have prevailed throughout much of Christian history, and this in turn implies a major educational task. Chapter 9 sets out suggestions of some ways in which the Church of England could address this – and Chapter 8 points out areas where there is still no consensus – but in this chapter seven areas of agreement can be identified.

1 the repudiation of antisemitism

The 1994 report *Christians and Jews: A New Way of Thinking* describes itself as 'a signpost' signalling

> the way to one of the most constructive developments in modern Christianity, its unequivocal rejection of antisemitism and its determination to reformulate its theology in such a way as no longer to give 'false witness' concerning the faith to which it is more intimately bound than all others.[1]

When Christians continue to repudiate antisemitism as strongly as they can, they need to be willing to listen carefully and humbly to any accusations – wherever they come from – of conscious or unconscious antisemitism expressed in words or actions. This is a particularly sensitive issue in relation to the current situation in the Middle East. On the one hand, robust criticism of the government or policies of Israel must clearly be a legitimate option, for Christians as much as for anybody else; on the other hand, it has to be acknowledged that 'anti-Zionism' has often been used as a respectable cloak for antisemitism.

2 the continuing vitality of Judaism

The 1988 Lambeth Conference document *Jews, Christians and Muslims: The Way of Dialogue* asserted: 'We firmly reject any view of Judaism which sees it as a fossil . . . Judaism is still a living religion, to be respected in its own right.'[2]

It is critically important for Christians to recognize that Jewish life and religion did not cease to develop in the first century of the Common Era, and that Judaism does not rely solely on the 'Old Testament'. It is also important to recognize that there is at least as much diversity among contemporary Jews as among Christians; genuine meeting can only be impeded by projecting onto Jewish people preconceived stereotypes, positive or negative. Christians further need to appreciate that Jewish–Christian relations are not the only, or necessarily the most important, issue for Jews today – the Jewish community also faces all the challenges of living in a society marked both by religious plurality and by widespread secularization.

3 the unacceptability of 'replacement theology'

The theory that the Christian Church has simply superseded or replaced the Jewish people, who no longer have any special place in God's calling, is widely seen to be untenable for a number of reasons. Theologically, it seems to call into question the faithfulness of God, 'who does not abandon those he calls' (*Jews, Christians and Muslims: The Way of Dialogue*). Scripturally, it fails to do justice to the subtlety of the New Testament witness regarding Israel, in particular to Paul's sustained reflections on his 'kindred according to the flesh'.[3] Historically, it inevitably led to the Christian accusations of Jews' 'God-forsakenness' which were at the root of the 'teaching of contempt'. Pastorally, a misunderstanding of the meaning of 'Old Testament' as 'out of date', 'outworn' or 'superseded' continues to feed negative attitudes to Judaism, and can cause grave offence to Jewish people, as well as diminishing Christian appreciation of the entire scope of the biblical witness. For these reasons, there is a growing feeling in some Christian circles that it is more appropriate to speak of the 'Hebrew Bible' rather than the 'Old Testament'.[4]

4 the need for education

It is widely recognized that a major educational task remains to be done in disseminating within the Church the findings of New Testament scholarship. Casually negative references to 'the Pharisees' in Christian preaching provide a clear example of this. The contribution of the Pharisaic movement to popular learning, their guardianship of the teaching of the Law and the prophets, their innovative character, their willingness to debate and discuss need to be understood and appreciated; from a Christian point of view, they can be seen to have a particular significance in that Jesus could be seen as engaging in debates within Pharisaism, rather than as rejecting the whole movement. More generally, there is a need to communicate to a wider audience the rich diversity of the Jewish contexts which form the background to the New Testament writings.

5 the Jewishness of Jesus

A particular emphasis of New Testament research – on the part of both Jewish and Christian scholars – has been a recovery of the Jewish identity of Jesus. Jesus was fully a man of his time and environment in first-century Palestine, and neither his teaching nor his ministry can be adequately understood except with reference to this contemporary Jewish life and religion. In fact, many of the sayings of Jesus can be paralleled by strikingly similar ones from other Jewish teachers. Recognition of this does not at all diminish the universal significance which Christians attribute to Jesus, but serves to ensure that that universality is always related to its particular, Jewish, context. It is particularly reprehensible to set 'the Jews' as a whole in opposition to Jesus as being those responsible for his death; historically, this downplays the role of the Roman authorities, while theologically responsibility for the crucifixion must be seen to fall on humanity as a whole.

6 sensitivity in liturgy

Christians need to be specially sensitive to references in the liturgy and in the public reading of Scripture which can be misunderstood or which can reinforce prejudices, and to the wording of prayers about the Jewish people. Texts which present particular problems are those referring to 'the Jews' or 'synagogues' in what may be described as derogatory terms, or passages highlighting conflict between the followers of Jesus and the established synagogue hierarchy.[5] Sensitive preaching on these can mitigate damage, by concentrating, for example, on 'human' traits rather than 'Jewish' ones. Care also needs to be taken with the mixture of texts appointed to be read together on any one day where, without guidance, preaching may focus on condemnation of Jews.[6] Other areas of sensitivity include: the choice of hymns; the way in which the expression 'the Old Testament' is used, and its relation to the New Testament developed in preaching and teaching; and the celebration by Christians of Passover meals and other observances, which are sometimes taken over from Jewish practice in ways which fail to honour the integrity of their original context.

7 sharing one hope: the kingdom of God

The 1988 Lambeth Conference document *Jews, Christians and Muslims: The Way of Dialogue* recognized the importance of the kingdom as a symbol shared by both Jews and Christians:

> Christians and Jews share one hope, which is for the realisation of God's Kingdom on earth. Together they wait for it, pray for it and prepare for it. This Kingdom is nothing less than human life and society transformed, transfigured and transparent to the glory of God. Christians believe that this glory has already shone in the face of Jesus Christ. In his life, death and resurrection the Kingdom of God, God's just rule, has already broken into the affairs of this world. Judaism is not able to accept this. However, Christian belief in Jesus is related to a frame of reference which Christians and Jews share. For it is as a result of incorporation into Jesus Christ that Christians came to share in the Jewish hope for the coming of God's Kingdom.

The document goes on to say that 'if this hope for God's Kingdom was given its central place by both Jews and Christians this would transform their relationship with one another'.[7] On such a basis of shared values, Jews and Christians can work together 'for social justice, respect for the rights of persons and nations, and social and international reconciliation' (Vatican, *Notes on Preaching and Catechesis*, 11). They will also recognize that Muslims, Hindus, Sikhs and members of other faith communities, as well as other people of good will, can in many situations be their partners in this work.

chapter 8
four areas of continuing debate among Christians

There are also important areas where currently no consensus exists, either among Christians or between Christians and Jews, and none seems likely to emerge within the foreseeable future. For informed and creative debate on these issues to continue both within the Church of England and in the ecumenical process, it is essential to recognize the diversity of views which are held in good faith. Four such areas of continuing debate are identified below.

1 the relationship between Christianity and Judaism

'A right understanding of the relationship with Judaism', says the Lambeth 1988 document, 'is fundamental to Christianity's own self-understanding.'[1] However, while a 'replacement' model may be generally rejected, there remains considerable disagreement among Christians as to how this relationship should be described. At least three different views can be identified.

a) one covenant

A single covenant is made with the people of God, in which Christians are able to share through Christ. Such a view builds on Romans 11.28-29: 'God's choice stands and they [the Jewish people] are his friends for the sake of the patriarchs. For the gracious gifts of God and his calling are irrevocable.' Paul van Buren is perhaps the best known among many Christian theologians who interpret the relation of the two faiths in light of this as the admission of Christians into the existing covenant with the Jews.[2]

b) two parallel covenants

Two parallel covenants are available for Jews and Christians. John Pawlikowski, for example, building on the suggestions of James Parkes, sees the two ways as equally valid expressions of the mercy and faithfulness of God. The first covenant, given at Sinai, is essentially communal, concerned with the life of the people as a whole and their day-to-day living on this earth. The second, given through Christ, is personal: people are called as individuals to a relationship with him which concerns not only this life but its fulfilment beyond space and time (Pawlikowski, 1982).

c) two totally different religions

Jacob Neusner is probably the most forcible proponent of the view that 'Judaism and Christianity are completely different religions, not different versions of one religion . . . They stand for different people talking about different things to different people.' On such a view, Christianity and Judaism have little more in common with one another than either of them does with other faiths (Neusner, 1991).

2 implications for Christology

Richard Harries explains how differences in understanding the relationship of the two religions affect Christological attitudes:

> Van Buren maintains that Jesus is only a man, albeit a man through whom God has worked to bring faith to the Gentile world. This approach affirms Judaism but it sits uneasily with historic Christianity. Pawlikowski, who is critical of van Buren's solution, stresses that Christianity is not simply a form of Judaism for Gentiles but it offers a belief in the Incarnation.

After drawing attention to the Jewish concept of God's dwelling with and in his people, Harries concludes:

> The problem of speaking of the Incarnation in relation to Judaism is the same as speaking of it at all. In order to speak, it is necessary to draw on continuity with other human experience. Yet if the Incarnation is unique, all models, metaphors and analogies break down. It may be that if Judaism and Christianity are both to retain their own recognisable self-identity, there are differences that have to be recognised rather than blurred. Genuine dialogue involves not only understanding and affirmation but bringing in to the relationship what is distinct and different.[3]

The exploration of Christology within the inter faith context represents an important challenge for Christians, in relation to other faiths as well as in dialogue with Judaism.

3 the Land

Christians hold differing views about the significance of the Land and the State of Israel today. The following two approaches differ fundamentally both in their methods of biblical interpretation and in their practical consequences.

i) The mainstream Christian view, at least since the time of Origen, has been to believe that *scriptural promises and prophecies concerning the Land are fulfilled in the coming of the kingdom of God in the person of Jesus*. This inevitably means that, however Christians try to interpret the return of Jews to the Land and the establishment of the State of Israel, they cannot understand these events as having any special significance in the coming of the kingdom. Any theology of the Land today needs therefore to be based on more general biblical principles about land, peoplehood and justice. A more radical development of this position would leave any theological interpretation on one side, insisting that present political realities should be addressed simply in terms of international law and human rights. Christian concern for justice in this situation has to address the rights of the Palestinian people as well as the security of Israel, and solidarity with Palestinian Christians in their plight makes this a particularly urgent issue.

ii) Other Christians rely on a literal exegesis of selected biblical texts to conclude that God's promise to Abraham and his descendants gives the Jewish people a divine right to the Land for all time, and that *predictions in the prophets about a return to the Land after exile have been fulfilled once again in the return of Jews to the land in the last 120 years*. Yet many would argue that this 'Christian Zionist' position relies on an approach to scriptural interpretation which takes little account either of recent scholarship or of contemporary political realities in the Middle East. A variant form is the position known as Christian millenarianism, which holds that the establishment of the State of Israel is a prelude to the end, when God will bring all Jews to Christ within his kingdom. Millenarianism is influential in American evangelical circles, and claims some support in this country and in Israel, particularly among those who point to the growing numbers of Messianic Jewish believers as evidence for the fulfilment of divine promises.

4 Christian mission and Jewish people

Christian 'mission' in relation to Jewish people has traditionally been thought of in terms of attempts to persuade them to come to faith in Jesus Christ. Such attempts have generally met with strenuous opposition from Jewish religious and community leaders. Contemporary Christian views about the possibility, morality, or wisdom of such missions 'to' Jews are very diverse; the three positions identified below are all represented within the Church of England today. At the same time, a broader and holistic understanding of the meaning of mission[4] opens for Christians the possibility of discerning a mission 'with' Jews to the world as a sharing in the work of God's kingdom,[5] though it would have to be recognized that most Jews would feel uncomfortable with the language of 'mission' in this context. There is also a very considerable range of opinion among Christians about the relation of proclamation to dialogue within the overall context of a holistic view of mission. Some see dialogue as the only appropriate context where witness to Christian faith can be made, while others distinguish proclamation and dialogue as distinct activities. There is a consensus among Christians, however, that it is wrong to use dialogue covertly as a cloak for proselytizing.

i)   Some within the Church of England today feel that *it is not appropriate for Christians to believe that they have any kind of 'mission to Jews'*. Often this view is based on a particular theological understanding of God's covenant with the Jewish people. Many further believe that Christian responsibility for the 'teaching of contempt', and therefore for anti-Judaism and antisemitism down the centuries, makes it unthinkable for Christians to seek to persuade Jews to change their minds about Jesus and 'become Christians'. The point is also strongly made that conversionist endeavours of this kind can destroy the foundations of trust between Christians and Jews, and so adversely affect the development of dialogue and cooperation which should be the imperative in Jewish–Christian relations. Christians should think in terms of 'a common mission' with Jews, in the sense that 'they share a mission to the world that God's name may be honoured, a common obligation to love God with their whole being and their neighbours as themselves'.[6]

ii)   Others feel that *it is entirely appropriate that Christians who establish relationships of genuine friendship and trust with Jews should continue to see these relationships in the context of Christian mission*. In open and frank dialogue they see no reason why Christians should not seek to share their beliefs about Jesus with Jews, provided they do so with genuine respect and sensitivity and carefully listen to what their Jewish friends have to share. There is no place, however, for special 'targeting' of Jews, still less for methods involving any kind of coercion or manipulation. In the history of our tragic past, the priority today must be to establish a new, constructive relationship with the Jewish people; this will mean trying to understand Judaism from a Jewish point of view, affirming common ground, but also sharing our most deeply held convictions even where this entails disagreement. Within this general understanding, some Christians find it possible to think in terms of *both* a common mission shared by Christians and Jews *and* a distinctive mission of Christians towards Jews. However, it is not evident that the possibility of such a position would be recognized by most Jewish people.

iii)   Yet others feel that **Christians have a responsibility to try to convince Jews about Jesus as Messiah**. This stems from the desire that they should become Jesus' disciples. Some would go further and say that, on the basis of Paul's conviction about the need to bring the gospel 'to the Jew first, and also to the Greek' (Romans 1.16), Christians have a special responsibility to evangelize Jews in particular, and this is likely to require special approaches directed to the Jewish community and taking account of their particular context and history. Jewish community leaders have expressed particularly vigorous objections to this approach, which is that generally promoted by Messianic Jewish believers. It should be noted that in 1992 the Archbishop of Canterbury, in declining an invitation to be Patron of the Church's Ministry among Jewish People[7] distanced himself from mission organizations entirely directed towards specific other faith communities. Among those committed to evangelism among Jewish people there is considerable debate about the appropriateness of particular forms of mission; CMJ, for example, have published their own 'Code of Practice' in this area.

chapter 9
some ways forward for the Church of England

The primary challenge for Christians in the area of Christian–Jewish relations is to engage in meeting, dialogue, and (where appropriate) practical cooperation with Jewish people. As members of the Church of England seek to do this alongside colleagues in other denominations, they will be greatly assisted by the existence, both nationally and at local branch level, of the Council of Christians and Jews. A number of other organizations are also active in this area; some are listed in Appendix 3, together with a small selection of the considerable quantity of literature and other resources available in Britain today. On an international level, the World Council of Churches is actively involved in promoting Christian–Jewish relations, and it is important for the Church of England to keep in touch with these conversations, and with the continuing work of the Vatican Commission for Religious Relations with the Jews.

While there is much that Christians and Jews can and should address together on a bilateral basis, there will also be areas where the involvement of people of other faith traditions is called for. On the one hand, multilateral exploration of shared spiritual values as a basis for practical inter faith cooperation in contemporary society should take into account all the major religions represented in Britain as well as Christianity and Judaism. Foundational work in this area has been done by the Inter Faith Network for the UK, the principal organization bringing together faith communities at a national level. The Church of England is involved in the Network through the Churches' Commission for Inter Faith Relations; the Board of Deputies of British Jews is also a Network member body. The Church of England is also represented, alongside other churches and the Jewish community, on the Inner Cities Religious Council, a body located in the Department of Environment, Transport and the Regions, which brings together representatives of those faith communities with a substantial presence in England's inner cities to work together with the Government in tackling the problems facing people in deprived urban areas.

On the other hand, Muslims, Jews and Christians may also have particular areas of trilateral shared concern, arising from their long interlocking histories, their current interaction in the Middle East, and the extent to which they share a common 'Abrahamic' heritage. These issues are of interest to the Three Faiths Forum, an organization established in 1997 on the initiative of Sir Sigmund Sternberg and Sheikh Dr Zaki Badawi; the Church of England continues to maintain informal contact with this Forum. Similarly, the International Council of Christians and Jews supports an Abrahamic Forum, and local three-faiths groupings are to be found in various places around Britain.

As well as this primary dialogue of Christians *with* Jews, the two preceding sections also demonstrate, in different ways, the need to strengthen conversations among Christians *about* Christian–Jewish relations. In areas such as covenant theology, Christology, attitudes to Israel (specifically to the land), and approaches to mission (see Chapter 8), it is clear that a significant range of strongly held views is and will continue to be held within the Church of England. It is important that Christians with differing standpoints on these topics listen carefully to one another, and also take into account the ways in which their debates are heard by people in the Jewish community. Christians of Jewish origin can have particularly important parts to play in this intra-Christian dialogue.

Equally, there is opportunity within the Church of England to build on the areas of consensus among Christians identified above (see Chapter 7). Liturgy and ministerial training are particularly important in forming attitudes in this respect, and in both some specific points could helpfully be addressed.

liturgy

i) Christians' views of Judaism and Jewish people are both formed and reinforced by forms of prayer and biblical exposition as experienced in worship – not only the textual content of liturgies as agreed centrally, but also the ways in which they are celebrated and interpreted at congregational level.

ii) In the Church's history, the most difficult liturgical elements for Christian–Jewish relations have been those of Holy Week – for example, the prayer for 'all Jews, Turks, Infidels and Hereticks' appointed in the *The Book of Common Prayer* for Good Friday. While alteration of that 1662 text is not practically feasible, the ongoing revision of seasonal liturgies needs to be sensitive to these issues, and to continue to build on the progress evident in *Lent, Holy Week, Easter* (1986).

29

iii) There has been a welcome recovery in lectionary provision at the Eucharist of readings from the 'Old Testament' (increasingly referred to as the 'Hebrew Scriptures'). The revision of lectionaries is a complex area, which operates under numerous constraints. One factor to bear in mind will be the way in which linking a passage from the Hebrew Bible to one from the New Testament can suggest a particular interpretation of the former. Special care needs to be taken that this relationship does not invite denigration or caricaturing of Jewish spirituality. This is an area where further detailed work could be helpful.

iv) As important as texts and terminology will be the ways in which liturgies are used, and particularly the ways in which those responsible locally for preaching and teaching interpret lectionary connections and expound the New Testament. There is thus a need for the Christian–Jewish relations dimension to be incorporated into planning for liturgical formation and education.

v) Further liturgical challenges facing Christians include provision of appropriate resources to mark the proposed Holocaust Day, and the growth of interest in many churches in adapting for Christian use the Passover *Seder* meal and other Jewish observances. Both cases raise sensitive issues about appropriate ways in which Christians can use Judaic resources in worship while respecting the integrity of their Jewish context. These are questions which should be addressed by Christians through the sharing of ideas and resources ecumenically.

ministerial training

i) Both training for ordination and Continuing Ministerial Education (CME) operate within a wider academic theological context in which Christian–Jewish relations have an increasingly high profile. They both also seek to equip people for ministry in a society marked by growing religious pluralism, of which Jewish communities form an important element in some places. It would be good to explore ways in which these two aspects of training could be strengthened; the following examples might be developed through a variety of learning methods and situations.

ii) New Testament studies (especially the Gospels and Paul) in recent decades have been transformed through recognition of the significance of the first-century Jewish context, and this is generally reflected in training for ordination. CME and other networks could be used to spread a wider awareness in the Church of current approaches to both the Hebrew Bible and the New Testament which take into account the Jewish experience. Consultations organized by the Church of England's Mission Theology Advisory Group have pointed to the advantages of an integral approach to the Bible in theological education, rather than splitting its study into discrete 'Old Testament' and 'New Testament' units (an approach which can easily lead to the marginalization of the former).

iii) Particular attention could be paid to twentieth-century developments in Christian–Jewish relations, and to reflection on the doctrinal, ecclesiological and missiological issues these raise. This might be promoted as a particularly significant contemporary issue in church history; there are a growing number of individuals and organizations able to offer specialized input on this subject.

iv) Engagement with Jewish communities and families in Britain can form a part of training for ministry and of CME in a multi-faith society. The geography of contemporary English Jewish demography is such that opportunities to meet Jewish people are only easily available in some parts of the country, yet an experiential sympathy with the wider issues involved in inter faith encounter can also be helped by meeting with Muslims, Hindus, Sikhs and people of other faith communities.

v) A critically important factor in forming attitudes to Jewish people among many clergy and ordinands may be a visit to Israel/Palestine. When organized in such a way as to meet a wide and informed range of people and groups, such visits can contribute tremendously towards awareness of the complexities of issues related to the Holy Land and its peoples; in other cases, they can serve simply to reinforce stereotypes with no serious engagement. Guidance to help prospective visitors or pilgrims choose wisely among the many options available would be helpful.

vi) There is a specific need to encourage a number of clergy and lay ministers to study Christian–Jewish relations in more depth, in order to build up a resource of well-informed ministry on these issues in the Church of England. The Centre for Jewish–Christian Relations in Cambridge and a number of other academic centres now offer distance learning courses and conference programmes in this area; it would be good for the Church to find ways to help develop the work of these centres through supporting participants in their programmes.

the background and nature of this document

This paper builds on a considerable tradition of Anglican and ecumenical reflection on Christian–Jewish relations, and it is itself the result of a long and detailed process of discussion and revision. The notes below summarize some of this history with special reference to personalities and events which have influenced the Church of England's involvement in these issues.

James Parkes (1896–1981) was an Anglican priest who became an authority on Judaism between the two world wars and is seen by many to have been a pioneer in developing Christian–Jewish understanding. In *The Conflict of the Church* and *the Synagogue* (1934) he explored the idea that Jews and Christians should think of themselves as belonging within two distinct covenants. In *End of an Exile: Israel, the Jews and the Gentile World* and *Whose Land: A History of the People of Palestine* he argued that the case for the State of Israel should not rest solely on the atrocities carried out in Europe, but on five principles, one of which was the continuity of Jewish people in the Holy Land down the centuries. He also recognized that injustices had been done to the Palestinians which would need to be redressed.

Nostra Aetate (28 October 1965). It is hard to exaggerate the significance of this document from the Second Vatican Council entitled *Declaration on the Relation of the Church to Non-Christian Religions*. After an introduction about Christian attitudes to other faiths in general, it urges members of the Roman Catholic Church 'to enter with prudence and charity into discussion and collaboration with members of other religions'. The following paragraph pleads for a new attitude towards Muslims in which all are asked to 'forget the past' and make every effort to 'achieve mutual understanding' and work to 'preserve and promote peace, liberty, social justice and moral values'.

The section on the Jews explains 'the spiritual ties which link the people of the New Covenant to the stock of Abraham', referring to verses like Galatians 3.7, Romans 9.4-5; 11.11-32 and Ephesians 2.14-16. On the basis of this 'common spiritual heritage' the Declaration does four things:

1. It encourages 'mutual understanding and appreciation' between Christians and people of other faiths.
2. It rejects the idea that Jews should be 'spoken of as rejected or accursed as if this followed from Holy Scripture'.
3. It condemns 'every form of persecution against whomsoever it may be directed' and 'all hatreds, persecutions, displays of antisemitism levelled at any time or from any source against the Jews'.
4. Finally it reminds the Church of its duty 'to proclaim the cross of Christ as the sign of God's universal love and the source of all grace'.

A later document, *Guidelines on Religious Relations with the Jews* (December 1974) builds on *Nostra Aetate* in four areas:

1. dialogue
2. liturgy
3. teaching and education, and
4. joint social action.

This was followed by *Notes for Preaching and Catechesis* (1985), and most recently by *We Remember: A Reflection on the Shoah* (1998). This corpus of four Vatican documents is helpfully presented in *Catholic Jewish Relations: Documents of the Holy See* (Catholic Truth Society, 1999). It is significant to note that the Vatican Commission for Religious Relations with the Jews falls under the Pontifical Council for Promoting Christian Unity, rather than the Pontifical Council for Inter-Religious Dialogue, which deals with relations with other faith traditions.

The Lambeth Conference 1988. The Bishop of Oxford, the Right Revd Richard Harries, and Rabbi Dr Norman Solomon led a working party which drafted a text for the Lambeth Conference about Christian–Jewish relations. In the discussion of the text, the Bishop in Jerusalem, the Right Revd Samir Kafity, insisted that Christian–Jewish relations could not be discussed without taking Islam into consideration. In consequence the document was rewritten and appeared as an Appendix, entitled *Jews, Christians and Muslims: The Way of Dialogue* in the final report (*The Truth Shall Make You Free*, Appendix 6, pp. 299–308).

In a section on 'The Way of Understanding' it points out particular areas in which Christians need to develop a deeper understanding of both Judaism and Islam. It commends 'The Way of Affirmation', encouraging Christians to be willing 'to affirm all they can affirm, especially when it resonates with the Gospel'. In describing 'The Way of Sharing', it explains that 'genuine dialogue demands that each partner brings to it the fullness of themselves and the tradition in which they stand' (p. 305). At the same time it must be recognized that 'Jews, Muslims and Christians have a common mission. They share a mission to the world that God's name may be honoured: "Hallowed be your name"' (p. 305). The document ends with a recommendation that an Inter Faith Committee should be set up which would among other things establish 'a common approach to people of other faiths on a Communion-wide basis' and appoint 'working parties to draw up more detailed guidelines for relationships with Judaism and Islam and other faiths as appropriate' (p. 308). These recommendations were included in Resolution 21 and passed by the Conference; the Anglican Communion's Network for Inter Faith Concerns (NIFCON) was subsequently charged by the 1998 Lambeth Conference with the monitoring of Christian–Muslim relations around the Communion, though currently NIFCON is still seeking adequate resourcing to fulfil this task.

Christians and Jews: A New Way of Thinking (CCIFR, 1994). The Church of England's Board for Mission and Unity (as it then was) asked its Inter Faith Consultative Group (IFCG) to consider how best to implement Lambeth Resolution 21. IFCG was clear that such work needed to be done ecumenically, and the BCC's Committee for Relations with People of Other Faiths (CRPOF) decided that a document for Christians was needed to express the sense of a new relationship between Christians and Jews, and a new way for Christians to think about Judaism. The Bishop of Oxford was consulted and agreed to chair a working party which included Rabbi Dr Norman Solomon, Sr Mary Kelly (Sisters of Sion), the Revd John Parry (URC) and Rabbi Tony Bayfield of the Reform Jewish tradition. The work was finally published by CRPOF's successor body, the Churches' Commission for Inter Faith Relations (CCIFR) after several years' gestation, due mainly to the transfer of responsibilities for inter faith matters.

The document, however, turned out to be controversial. CCIFR was in the unenviable position of being asked to approve a text which it had played no part in producing, since very few members of CRPOF continued as members of CCIFR. The continuing but outgoing Moderator, David Silk, felt that he owed it to the authors to proceed with publication after so long a period of preparation, but some voices in the Commission thought that Christian antisemitism was not sufficiently recognized in the text, not least the antisemitism of the New Testament itself. Others felt passionately that in the brief passage about the State of Israel the Palestinian case had not been adequately stated. Publication went ahead, however, despite these misgivings.

When the Secretary of IFCG brought this ecumenical document to the Board of Mission there was further criticism. Within the Partnership for World Mission (a part of the Board of Mission), concern over certain aspects of the document was expressed by representatives of the Church's Ministry among Jewish People (CMJ), Crosslinks and others. The Board agreed to send the document to the House of Bishops, where several members again were unhappy about its treatment of mission, particularly the statement that 'Jews and Christians have a mission in common'. The bishops left it to the discretion of individual bishops to circulate it in their own dioceses.

the Archbishop of Canterbury and CMJ. In 1992 Dr Carey became the first Archbishop of Canterbury for 150 years to decline the usual invitation from the Church's Ministry among Jewish People (CMJ) to be their Patron. He is *ex officio* a co-President of the Council of Christians and Jews, but previous Archbishops have found it possible to hold both offices. Dr Carey noted in his letter to CMJ that he was committed to 'the Gospel for all people', but that in contemporary circumstances it was necessary for an Archbishop of Canterbury to be also a protector of religious freedom for all. His need to build up the trust of the Jewish community would not be helped by close association with an organization 'entirely directed towards another faith community'.

the CCJ Code. The Council of Christians and Jews was formed in 1942 as an initiative of Chief Rabbi Dr Joseph Hertz and Archbishop William Temple to inform, educate and encourage tolerance and respect, and it remains a forum for both Jews and Christians to come together in a spirit of trust and reconciliation. It is not, therefore, an exclusively Christian organization and has no unifying theology, merely an agreed approach.

In August 1996 CCJ completed and published a 'Code of Practice for Members'. This was drawn up in response to a request from the Presidents of CCJ and was concerned to preserve an atmosphere of trust between Christian and Jewish members to enable dialogue and discussion to continue under its auspices. It involved extensive consultation at all levels over a period of eighteen months, including senior figures in the Anglican Communion.

Considerable attention was paid to this Code of Practice in the Christian press, particularly to two passages:

Insensitive comments about Christianity or Judaism, or attempts to use CCJ for missionary activity, destroy the mutual trust that is essential to our work.

Aggressive proselytism is always wrong and if this or any unsuitable behaviour is reported to CCJ, appropriate action will be taken.

Questions were asked about the nature of mission and whether a Christian should desist from missionary activity in any situation. CMJ also took exception to the phrase: 'Concern will not be confined to behaviour within the CCJ.'

concerns of Jewish Christians. As a result of this public debate about the CCJ Code of Practice, the late Revd Michael Vasey put the following question to the Chairman of the Board of Mission at General Synod in November 1996:

In view of recent statements issuing from the Council of Christians and Jews, what plans does the Board have to express the Church of England's support for those of its members who see themselves as both Jewish and Christian, and to affirm their active involvement in sharing the Good News of the Messiah with their fellow Jews?

The Board of Mission recognized that while the question of support for a particular ethnic group of Christians lies properly within the remit of the Committee for Minority Ethnic Anglican Concerns, questions concerning mission to people of other faiths, and definitions of 'Jewish' and 'Christian', should be addressed to the Inter Faith Consultative Group (IFCG).

the present paper. In response to Michael Vasey's question, IFCG established a working group to attempt a feasibility study to identify the fundamental issues in the debate. The members of this working group were: the Revd Colin Chapman (Director of 'Faith to Faith' Consultancy; Chair), the Revd Canon Dr Christopher Lamb (at that time Secretary of IFCG), Dr Jenny Sankey (Lecturer in Doctrine), the Revd Dr David Rayner (Vicar of the Resurrection, Smethwick), and the Revd Dr Walter Riggans (General Director, CMJ, until 31 October 1998).

When a first draft of this paper was presented to the Board of Mission in 1998, it was noted that issues arising from the position of Jewish Christians could not be isolated from the wider context of Christian–Jewish relations. The Board requested that the document be revised to deal more adequately with this broader agenda, bearing in mind work that had already been done in this field. The Revd Colin Chapman agreed to undertake this revision in collaboration with the Revd Canon Dr Michael Ipgrave (by then Secretary of IFCG), and in consultation with the Bishop of Oxford, the Bishop of Rochester, the Council of Christians and Jews, and the Revd Dr Walter Riggans. The revised paper was endorsed by the Board in June 1999, and discussed by the House of Bishops in January 2000. The bishops referred back the question of the paper's publication to the Board. At the same time, they expressed the hope that ways could be found to carry forward discussion within the Church of England of the issues it raised, and to continue the development of training, liturgical and other resources for Christian–Jewish relations.

Following this, it was agreed that the paper should be published, with revisions both in the light of the bishops' discussion and also bearing in mind comments from two ecumenical expert referees (the Revd Dr Martin Forward and the Revd Jonathan Dean). The Revd Canon Dr Michael Ipgrave and Dr Anne Davison, on behalf of the Inter Faith Consultative Group, then embarked on a further revision of the text on this basis, and the paper in its present form was published in spring 2001.

It can thus be seen that this document represents the latest stage in a long and complex process which has involved people from a wide diversity of viewpoints within the Church of England and beyond. It has no authority other than that of an occasional paper published to summarize the issues, to encourage discussion, and to suggest ways of promoting good practice within the Church of England.

Messianic congregations and the traditional churches

The following two sets of questions[1] have been compiled by the Revd Dr Walter Riggans, formerly General Director of the Church's Ministry among Jewish People.

1 questions about Messianic congregations

The increase in the number of Messianic Jews and Messianic Jewish fellowships or congregations in recent years (some of which have links with Anglican churches in different countries) raises a number of questions in the minds of Christians in the traditional churches:

- If Messianic Jews believe that Jesus the Messiah has 'destroyed the barrier, the dividing wall of hostility' between Jews and Gentiles and has created 'one new man out of the two' (Ephesians 2.14-15), what are their reasons for wanting to create fellowships or churches mainly or exclusively for Jewish Christians? Is it to do with liturgical preferences, or with the desire to belong to a homogeneous group? Is it to create a setting to which other Jews can more easily be invited?
- Are such congregations formed mainly from those formerly identified as Jews (and their families) who wish to continue worship using familiar traditions? If significant numbers of Gentiles are joining, why are they doing this? Could such Gentiles be properly described as Messianic Jews if they belong to a Messianic Jewish congregation?
- Are those aspects of Jewish law which Christians consider redundant for them (e.g. laws of *Kashrut*, observance of Yom Kippur) still practised? If so, what is the rationale for this?
- Is the theology of Messianic Jews recognizably Trinitarian? If not, is it important that it should be?
- Do Messianic Jewish congregations have any desire to worship and cooperate with Christians of other traditions?
- When such groups have links with Anglican churches, what are the ecclesiological issues raised? Is there anything distinctive in

Anglican ecclesiology that makes it possible to find ways of understanding and developing these relationships?

● Are Messianic Jews sensitive to the concerns of others within the Hebrew community about particular methods of evangelizing Jews?

2 questions about traditional churches

Part of the contemporary reluctance of Messianic Jews to embrace the term 'Christian' in their self-definitions lies in their shock, shared with all Jews, that people calling themselves Christians, often church leaders at the highest levels, have been responsible for so much hatred and violence aimed at Jewish people and their heritage. The Holocaust has especially traumatized Messianic Jewish believers as much as any other Jews.

● How can churches best respond to the challenge of these brothers and sisters in the faith who need to know what caused such antisemitism, and who need to be reassured that it is being rooted out of churches and the lives of Christians today?

Another part of the reluctance arises from the fear of being identified with the long-standing tradition that Jewish people must jettison their Jewishness on every level when they become followers of Jesus. This new determination to be accepted as still being Jewish is an affirmation of Jewish identity.

● How can churches best develop a welcoming of the Jewishness of Messianic Jewish believers?

A third reluctance relates to the historic factor of forced conversions and false professions of faith in Jesus, by Jewish people trying either to escape persecution or to further their careers in a dreadfully prejudiced European society. The phrase 'Jewish Christian' conjures up images of such 'conversions'; and Messianic Jews are keen to let it be known that their faith is based on conviction alone.

● How can churches best respond to this challenge from Messianic Jewish communities?

appendix 3

some resources

printed material

A vast and ever-growing quantity of printed material is available in all the areas discussed in this report. The list below includes all the books listed in the text, together with one or two suggestions for further reading. Neither inclusion nor exclusion of any book should be taken to imply any judgement on its value.

Several extensive bibliographies, some of them annotated, can be found at the 'Christian–Jewish Relations' web page listed on page 45.

Church statements

Marcus Braybrooke (ed.), *Jews and Christians: What do the Churches Say?*, Council of Christians and Jews, 1992.

Allan Brockway, Rolf Rendtorff, Simon Schoon and Paul van Buren (eds), *The Theology of the Churches and the Jewish People: Statements by the World Council of Churches and its Member Churches*, World Council of Churches Publications, 1988.

Churches' Commission for Inter Faith Relations, *Christians and Jews: A New Way of Thinking*, Council of Churches for Britain and Ireland, 1994.

Helga Croner (ed.), *Stepping Stones to Further Jewish–Christian Relations*, Stimulus Books, Paulist Press, 1977.

Helga Croner (ed.), *More Stepping Stones to Jewish–Christian Relations*, Stimulus Books, Paulist Press, 1985.

Eugene J. Fisher (ed.), *Catholic Jewish Relations: Documents from the Holy See*, Catholic Truth Society, 1999.

Lambeth Conference 1988, 'Jews, Christians and Muslims: The Way of Dialogue', Appendix 6 in *The Truth Shall Make You Free*, Church House Publishing, 1988.

interpreting the Bible

Gregory Baum, *Is the New Testament Anti-Semitic?: A Re-examination of the New Testament*, Paulist Press, 1965.

Marcus Braybrooke, *Time to Meet: Towards a Deeper Relationship Between Jews and Christians*, SCM Press, 1990.

Walter Brueggemann, *Old Testament Theology: Essays on Structure, Themes and Text*, Fortress Press, 1992.

James Charlesworth, *Jesus within Judaism: New Light from Exciting Archaeological Discoveries*, Crossroad, 1991.

James Dunn, *The Partings of the Ways Between Christianity and Judaism and Their Significance for the Character of Christianity*, SCM Press, 1988.

Jules Isaac, *Jesus and Israel*, (English translation), Holt, Rinehart and Winston, 1971.

Jules Isaac, *The Teaching of Contempt: Christian Roots of Anti-Semitism*, (English translation), Holt, Rinehart and Winston, 1964.

Graham Keith, *Hated Without a Cause? A Survey of Anti-Semitism*, Paternoster Press, 1997.

Gareth Lloyd-Jones, *Hard Sayings: Difficult New Testament Texts for Jewish–Christian Dialogue*, Council of Christians and Jews, 1993.

Hyam Maccoby, *Jewish Views of Jesus*, Middlesex University Centre for Inter-Faith Dialogue, 1995.

Rosemary Radford Ruether, *Faith and Fratricide: The Theological Roots of Antisemitism*, Seabury Press, 1974.

Walter Riggans, *Yeshua ben David*, Monarch, 1995

Krister Stendahl, *Paul Among Jews and Gentiles*, Fortress Press, 1976.

Geza Vermes, *Jesus the Jew: A Historian's Reading of the Gospels*, William Collins, 1973.

Tom Wright, *The New Testament and the People of God* (*Christian Origins and the Question of God*, Vol. 1), SPCK, 1992.

Tom Wright, *Jesus and the Victory of God (Christian Origins and the Question of God*, Vol. 2), SPCK, 1993.

antisemitism in history

Jeremy Cohen (ed.), *Essential Papers on Judaism and Christianity in Conflict: From Late Antiquity to Reformation*, New York University Press, 1991.

Dan Cohn-Sherbok, *The Crucified Jew: Twenty Centuries of Christian Anti-Semitism*, Fount, 1993.

Edward Flannery, *The Anguish of the Jews: Twenty-three Centuries of Antisemitism*, Paulist Press, 1985.

Bernard Lewis, *Semites and Anti-Semites: An Inquiry into Conflict and Prejudice*, Phoenix House, 1986.

Runnymede Commission on Antisemitism, *A Very Light Sleeper: The Persistence and Dangers of Antisemitism*, Runnymede Trust, 1994.

Vatican Commission for Religious Relations with the Jews, 'Notes on the Correct Way to Present the Jews and Judaism in Preaching and Catechesis in the Roman Catholic Church' (1985), in Eugene J. Fisher (ed.), *Catholic Jewish Relations: Documents from the Holy See*, Catholic Truth Society, 1999.

the Holocaust

Emil Fackenheim, *To Mend the World: Foundations of Future Jewish Thought*, Schocken Books, 1982.

Martin Gilbert, *The Holocaust : A History of the Jews of Europe During the Second World War*, HarperCollins, 1987

Deborah Lipstadt, *Denying the Holocaust: The Growing Assault on Truth and Memory*, Penguin, 1994.

Carol Rittner, Stephen Smith, and Irena Steinfeldt (eds), *The Holocaust and the Christian World: Reflections on the Past – Challenges for the Future*, Kuperard, 2000.

Vatican Commission for Religious Relations with the Jews, 'We Remember: A Reflection on the Shoah' (1998), in Eugene J. Fisher (ed.), *Catholic Jewish Relations: Documents from the Holy See*, Catholic Truth Society, 1999.

British Judaism today

Geoffrey Alderman, *Modern British Jewry*, Oxford University Press, 1998.

Stephen Brook, *The Club: The Jews of Modern Britain*, Constable, 1989.

Vivian Lipman, *A History of the Jews in Britain Since 1858*, Holmes and Meier, 1990.

Jonathan Sacks, *A Letter in the Scroll: Understanding Our Jewish Identity and Exploring the Legacy of the World's Oldest Religion*, Free Press, 2000.

Christian–Jewish relations

Paul van Buren, *Theology of the Jewish–Christian Reality*, Harper & Row, 1980–88.

Robert Everett, *Christianity without Anti-Semitism: James Parkes and the Jewish Christian Encounter*, Pergamon Press, 1993.

Helen Fry, *Christian–Jewish Dialogue: A Reader*, University of Exeter Press, 1996.

Michael Hilton, *The Christian Effect on Jewish Life*, SCM Press, 1994.

Jacob Neusner, *Jews and Christians: The Myth of a Common Tradition*, SCM Press, 1991.

John Pawlikowski, *Christ in the Light of the Jewish–Christian Dialogue*, Paulist Press, 1982.

Marc Saperstein, *Moments of Crisis in Jewish–Christian Relations*, SCM Press, 1989.

Vatican Commission for Religious Relations with the Jews, 'Guidelines and Suggestions for Implementing the Conciliar Declaration *Nostra Aetate* (no. 4)' (1974), in Eugene J. Fisher (ed.), *Catholic Jewish Relations: Documents from the Holy See*, Catholic Truth Society, 1999.

Jewish believers in Jesus

Dan Cohn-Sherbok, *Messianic Judaism: The First Study of Messianic Judaism by a Non-Adherent*, Continuum, 2000.

John Fieldsend, *Messianic Jews: Challenging Church and Synagogue*, Monarch, 1993.

Arnold Fruchtenbaum, *Hebrew Christianity: Its Theology, History and Philosophy*, Ariel, 1983.

Michele Guinness, *A Little Kosher Seasoning*, Hodder & Stoughton, 1994

Carol Harris-Shapiro, *Messianic Judaism: A Rabbi's Journey through Religious Change in America*, Beacon Press, 1999.

Hugh Montefiore, *On Being a Jewish Christian: Its Blessings and Its Problems*, Hodder & Stoughton, 1998.

David Stern (tr.), *Complete Jewish Bible*, Olive Press, 1998.

David Stern, *Jewish New Testament Commentary*, Olive Press, 1992.

organizations

Those in Britain mentioned in the text can be contacted as follows:

Board of Deputies of British Jews, Commonwealth House, 1–19 New Oxford Street, LONDON, WC1A 1NU; www.bod.org.uk

Centre for Jewish–Christian Relations, Wesley House, Jesus Lane, CAMBRIDGE, CB5 8BJ; www.cjcr.org.uk

Churches' Commission for Inter Faith Relations, Church House, Great Smith St, LONDON, SW1P 3NZ; www.ctbi.org.uk/ccifr

Church's Ministry among Jewish People, 30c Clarence Road, ST ALBANS, Herts AL1 4JJ; www.cmj.org.uk

Council of Christians and Jews, 5th Floor, Camelford House, 89 Albert Embankment, LONDON, SE1 7TP; www.ccj.org.uk

Inner Cities Religious Council, Department of the Environment, Transport and the Regions, Eland House, Bressenden Place, LONDON, SW1E 5DU; www.detr.gov.uk

Inter Faith Network for the UK, 5–7 Tavistock Place, LONDON, WC1H 9SN; www.interfaith.org.uk

Three Faiths Forum, Star House, 104–108 Grafton Rd, LONDON, NW5 4BD.

web pages

The following are very informative:

Beth Shalom Holocaust Centre: www.bethshalom.com

Christian–Jewish Relations: www.jcrelations.net/index.htm

Institute for Jewish Policy Research: www.jpr.org.uk

International Council of Christians and Jews: www.iccj.org

Judaism and Jewish Resources: shamash.org/trb/judaism.html

The Nizkor Project: www.nizkor.org

The Roman Curia – Pontifical Councils:
www.vatican.va/roman_curia/pontifical_councils/index.htm

World Council of Churches Interreligious Relations:
wcc-coe.org/wcc/what/interreligious/index-e.html

notes

introduction

1. In accordance with contemporary scholarly usage, the unhyphenated form of the word (antisemitism) is used throughout this report to indicate prejudice against and hatred of Jewish people, in preference to the more traditional hyphenated form (anti-Semitism). As 'Semites' describes most of the people of south-west Asia and north-east Africa, the latter can give rise to various incongruities – for example, the rather circular argument that 'No Arab can be anti-Semitic since Arabs are themselves Semites.'

chapter 1: the historical and theological context

1. It is indeed possible to argue that the issues highlighted by the coming of Christianity are in fact present throughout the earlier biblical record. For example, Walter Brueggemann points to an ambivalence between, on one hand, a 'core tradition' which unites the promise of God with Abraham, the people Israel, and the land of Israel, and on the other, a 'counter testimony' which raises serious doubts about such a unity (Brueggemann, 1992). Brueggemann's analysis – developed from a study of Jewish commentators – shows how the Hebrew scriptures could be seen as providing a way in for the New Testament claim that Abraham is father of Jew and Gentile alike.

2. This also led to a transformation of traditional doctrine for some in the Christian tradition – for example, some of the early Unitarians in eastern Europe were influenced by contemporary Jewish teachings.

3. The first recorded instance of the accusation was at Norwich in 1144 (the death of 'Saint' William); a similar allegation was made at Blois in 1171, for example.

4. For the meaning of this expression, see Chapter 2, para. 3.

chapter 2: the New Testament

1. *Christians and Jews: A New Way of Thinking*, p. 2.

2. Lloyd-Jones, 1993, p. 39f.

chapter 3: antisemitism

1. In contemporary Russia, for example, nationalistic antisemitism often presents itself as a defence of that Russian identity of which Orthodoxy is an indispensable component. Some church leaders have colluded with, and a few have encouraged, this approach; on the other hand, Patriarch Aleksii II has firmly denounced attacks on synagogues, and has spoken positively of the Old Testament heritage which links Christians and Jews.

2. However, following the forcible baptism of thousands of Jews in Spain and Portugal in the fifteenth and sixteenth centuries (thousands more were expelled at this time), religiously based prejudice against the converts ('New Christians') provided the basis for racial discrimination against all those who could not establish 'purity of blood' (*limpieza de sangre*), i.e. those who were suspected of Jewish antecedents, and by implication of the continuing covert practice of Judaism.

3. When Hitler visited the 1934 performance, he was proudly told by the village mayor: 'We are presenting the most antisemitic play ever.' The traditional text, by Father Alois Daisenberger (1860), referred to 'the accursed Jews'.

4. As the Pope's words were in the form of a prayer, 'your' here of course refers to God.

chapter 4: the Holocaust

1. Peter Cullen, 'A Guide to *We Remember . . .*' – briefing paper on CCJ web site (see Appendix 3).

2. *Memory and Reconciliation: The Church and the Faults of the Past*, produced in December 1999 by the International Theological Commission of the Congregation of the Faith, on the Vatican web site at http://www.vatican.va/roman_curia/congregations/cfaith/documents/rc_con_cfaith_doc_20000307_memory-reconc-itc_en.html. See Chapter 3, last paragraph.

3. The complete text of this judgement is available on, for example, the web site of The Nizkor Project, at http://www.nizkor.org/hweb/people/i/irving-david/judgment-00-00.html.

chapter 5: the State of Israel

1. See Chapter 8, section 3 'The Land'.

chapter 6: Jewish people who believe in Jesus

1. This attitude does not necessarily extend to Jews who recognize other figures as the Messiah – for example, those within the Lubavitch tradition who accept the Rebbe Menachem Schneersohn as Messiah are generally still regarded as authentically Jewish by their fellow Jews.

2. There are interesting reflections on the status of Messianic Jews in the light of these identity issues in two recent sympathetic studies by (non-Messianic) rabbis: Harris-Shapiro, 1999, and Cohn-Sherbok, 2000.

3. See Chapter 8, section 4 'Christian mission and Jewish people'.

chapter 7: seven areas of agreement among Christians

1. *Christians and Jews: A New Way of Thinking*, p. 3.

2. *Jews, Christians and Muslims: The Way of Dialogue*, para. 14.

3. Romans 9–11. These chapters also seem difficult to relate to some other models of the relationship of Judaism and Christianity – for example, 'two covenants' or 'two

separate religions' (see Chapter 8, section 1 'The relationship between Christianity and Judaism').

4. Even this terminology has a problematic side, however, in that it does not incorporate the 'deuterocanonical' books, which were transmitted only through the Greek of the Septuagint. An alternative which is occasionally used is 'First Testament'.

5. e.g. Revelation 2.9-10; John 8.31,44; Matthew 27.24-25.

6. e.g. Martyrdom of Stephen, 'They shall put you out of the synagogues' (John 16.2); Feast of Christ the King, where congregations are invited to consider Christ's kingship in the context of a reading centring on the inscription 'King of the Jews'.

7. *Jews, Christians and Muslims: The Way of Dialogue*, paras 14, 15.

chapter 8: four areas of continuing debate among Christians

1. *Jews, Christians and Muslims: The Way of Dialogue*, para. 13.

2. Van Buren, 1980; his later thought, however, suggests a plurality of covenants, one with every different cultural-religious grouping.

3. Richard Harries, unpublished paper. We are grateful for permission to quote from this paper.

4. The 'Five Marks of Mission', originally developed by the Anglican Consultative Council, were adopted by the Church of England's General Synod in 1996. They are as follows: 1. To proclaim the good news of the kingdom; 2. To teach, baptize and nurture new believers; 3. To respond to human need by loving service; 4. To seek to transform the unjust structures of society; 5. To strive to safeguard the integrity of creation and sustain and renew the life of the earth.

5. See Chapter 7, section 7 'Sharing one hope: the kingdom of God'.

6. *Jews, Christians and Muslims: The Way of Dialogue*, para. 27.

7. See Appendix 1, 'The Archbishop of Canterbury and CMJ'.

appendix 2: Messianic congregations and the traditional churches

1. See Chapter 6, last paragraph.

index

Note: Where more than one sequence of notes appears on the same page, references to the notes take the form '1a', '2d', indicating the first note 1 or the fourth note 2 on that page.